Theme 4

MW00565579

HOUGHTON MIFFLIN
Reading
A Legacy of Literacy

Person to Person

HOUGHTON MIFFLIN

BOSTON • MORRIS PLAINS, NJ

California • Colorado • Georgia • Illinois • New Jersey • Texas

Design, Art Management and Page Production: Kirchoff/Wohlberg, Inc.

ILLUSTRATION CREDITS
4-10, 12-25 Nancy Carpenter. **26-33, 35-47** Amanda Harvey. **48-69** Ann Boyajian. **70-74, 76-77, 79-91** Mark Elliott.

Printed in U.S.A.

ISBN: 0-618-04410-8

456789-VH-05 04 03 02 01

Person to Person

Contents

Something for Everyone

by Joanne Korba
illustrated by Nancy Carpenter

Strategy Focus

Tony, Jay, and Elvis choose music for a neighborhood party. As you read, **predict** what their choices will be and **infer** how the party will turn out.

Everyone who lives in the Santiagos' neighborhood calls it the UN — the United Nations. That's because the neighbors come in all colors and nationalities. English is spoken here. But so are Chinese, Portuguese, Russian, Haitian Creole, Laotian, and more than one kind of Spanish.

Every summer, the UN has a big neighborhood party. There's always lots of food, fun, and friendship. Neighbors take turns being in charge. Last summer it was the Santiagos' turn.

"Then we're agreed," Mrs. Santiago was saying over the phone. "We'll have the party at the end of July. It's going to be great this year! We'll talk more later, *amiga*."

As she hung up, her son Tony walked into the kitchen. He was followed by his best friend, Jay. "You're looking at one-half of this year's UN Party Committee," Mrs. Santiago announced proudly. "I just asked your mother to be the other half," she said to Jay. "These parties are getting too big for one family to manage."

Tony Santiago and Jay Kovak had been best friends since they were in preschool. Now they were 11 years old and in the same sixth-grade class. They were on the same Little League team, and they played for the same after-school hockey team. They liked the same computer games and read the same books.

Their parents were friends too. It made sense for the Santiagos and Kovaks to work together on the neighborhood party.

"What about Papi?" Tony asked his mother.
"Isn't he doing anything for the party?"

"We put him in charge of the barbecues," his
mother answered. "Along with Jay's dad."

"Hey, a Santiago and a Kovak should be in charge
of music, too!" said Tony, pointing to himself and Jay.
"*We* know what's hot and what's not."

"M-m-m-m," his mother answered. She looked doubtful. But after a few silent moments, she said, "Okay. But just remember — the music is meant to entertain people. To make them sing and dance and enjoy themselves. That's the point."

Jay nodded. "Sure, sure, Mrs. Santiago," he said. "We can do that." He turned to Tony. "Come on! Let's go to my house and figure out what music we want to use."

The boys headed for the door. "Tony!" Mrs. Santiago called out sweetly. "Haven't you forgotten something?"

Tony stopped and sighed. He'd almost managed to escape.

"Come on, Tony. You know you're supposed to look after your brother in the afternoon. I have to work in peace." Mrs. Santiago wrote an advice column for a local paper. "We agreed!" she said.

"Yeah. I know, Mami," Tony answered. He sighed again as he walked into the hall. "Elvis!" he called. "Come on down! We're going over to Jay's."

Then he leaned against the wall, waiting. And waiting. And waiting.

His brother took his time coming downstairs. He didn't like the afternoon babysitting arrangement any better than his brother did. "I just happen to be reading a really good book," Elvis complained. "Why do I have to stop and go to Jay's?"

"Because we're in charge of the dance music for the neighborhood party," Tony said. "Jay and I have to decide what to tape. But hey, bring your book. You can read while we have our meeting."

Elvis's eyes lit up. "*We're* in charge of the dance music? Cool! I know all about dance music. I'm a great dancer. You two can just leave it all to me!" He ran out the door, heading for Jay's house.

"No, no, you've got it wrong. It's just Jay and me! Hey . . . wait!" Tony called, dashing down the sidewalk after Elvis.

Jay followed the pair, shaking his head. He was pretty sure that the first meeting of the UN Dance Music Committee wasn't going to go well.

They all sat on the floor of the sunporch that Jay used as a bedroom. Tony looked through his friend's CDs. Jay had a notepad in his lap. "We should make a list of the music we want to tape," he said to Tony. He was trying to ignore Elvis. "How many tapes should we make?"

Before Tony could answer, Elvis started talking. "We have to tape music that people can really dance to. That means Latin music. Everyone knows it has the best dance beat." He got up and started dancing to an imaginary song.

"Don't you have a book to read?" was all Tony said to Elvis.

But Jay was ready to argue. "Well, *this* everyone doesn't agree. If we're talking about great dance music, I have some techno albums that are perfect!"

"Okay, that's set. Latin music and techno music," Tony said soothingly. "Great. I think this meeting is going really well. . . . "

"Techno? You mean that computer junk?" Elvis sniffed. "That's not real music!"

"Excuse me?" Jay said coldly.

Jay and Elvis glared at each other. Tony got between them. "Hey, hey," he said. "Why make this an argument between two kinds of music? Why can't we have both? In fact, we should have all different kinds of music — rock, country, rap, hip-hop. . . . "

"Rap and hip-hop are the same thing," Elvis mumbled.

"No, they're not," Tony said firmly, although he wasn't sure. "Anyway, the point is that for the United Nations party, we need United Nations music."

"That's true," Jay said, nodding. "Music from other countries."

"Latin music is from other countries," Elvis mumbled. He frowned down at the floor, thinking. Suddenly, he looked up.

"There's something else we have to remember," Elvis told Tony and Jay. "We can't just have dance music that kids like. We need to make sure that we have music our parents like. And older people too!"

Jay caught on. "Right! We need some disco and funk. Mambos. Cha-chas. And swing music, for that kind of dance they did in the old days. . . . "

"You mean the jitterbug?" Elvis asked.

"Yeah!" cried Jay. "Now we'll really have something for everyone."

17

"But . . ." Tony began. Two heads swiveled toward him. Tony didn't agree? How could Tony have a problem? He was always the peacemaker.

"How do *we* know what kind of dance music everyone likes?" Tony asked. "Maybe there's Chinese dance music that we don't know about. And Brazilian music. Then there's Mr. Bromley. What kind of music do you suppose *he* likes?"

Mr. Bromley spent most of his time on his front porch, frowning at everyone who passed by. He usually greeted Jay and Tony with "You kids stay off my grass!"

"Mr. Bromley!" said Elvis. "He won't dance no matter what we play! You *can't* think of something for every single person in the neighborhood."

"I guess maybe that's true," Jay said.

"No, it's not!" Tony shot back. He was smiling. "I have a plan."

Tony's plan was to ask every person in the
neighborhood — every man, woman, and child
(except really little kids) — to give him a recording of
their favorite dance tune. Then he and Jay could put
all the tunes on tape.

With the help of Elvis and two of his friends, they
carried out the plan quickly. House by house, they
gathered armloads of music. There were 50-year-old
records, 25-year-old tapes, and brand-new CDs. They
had enough music to make dance tapes for five years'
worth of parties!

"So you admit it," Mrs. Santiago said when the tapes were finished. "Your little brother was a big help to you."

"Let's not get carried away, Mami," said Tony. "He started off by being a big *pain*." His mother put her hands on her hips. "Okay, okay!" Tony said. "In the end, he was kind of a help. Maybe a pretty big help. All right, all right. We couldn't have done it without him!" He sighed.

His mother patted his cheek. "You're a good big brother," she said.

That year, the UN party was hot in every way. The Fourth of July sun was hot. Hamburgers, turkey burgers, fish, steaks, chicken, and ribs sizzled hot and smoky on the grill. And most of all, there was the dance music. It was hot, hot, hot!

Because there was something for everyone on the dance tape, everyone danced. Every man, woman, and child in the UN. *Everybody.*

Even Mr. Bromley.

Responding

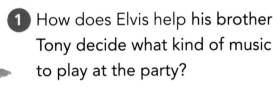

Think About the Selection

1. How does Elvis help his brother Tony decide what kind of music to play at the party?

2. Why do Tony and Jay decide to play many different kinds of music?

3. Making a big party can be a problem for one person. What does Tony's mom do about that?

Find Solutions

Copy the chart on a piece of paper. Read Tony and Jay's problem. Write solutions you read about in the story. Then circle the one you think is the best.

Problem	Solutions
Tony and Jay have to decide what music to tape for the party.	1. Tape music people can really dance to. 2. ? 3. ?

PRETTY COOL, FOR A CAT

by **Kitty Colton**
illustrated by **Amanda Harvey**

Strategy Focus

Toby is an amusing pet. As you read, **monitor** and **clarify** your understanding of how animals can help people feel better.

I'd been wanting a dog since — well, since I could say the word *dog*. According to Mom, I learned to say "dog" even before I said "Mom" or "Dad."

I never got one, though. My parents said, "Too much work." Still, every year, especially around my birthday, I begged them.

When I was really little, I got stuffed dogs. A lot of them. My bedroom was like a kennel without the barks. Then my parents tried to interest me in other pets. First it was a mouse, then a turtle, then a goldfish. All very nice and very easy to take care of, according to my parents. And all very, very boring.

The October before my ninth birthday, I started up the same old whine. "Ple-e-e-a-s-e can I get a dog this year?" I begged. "I will totally take care of him. You won't even know he's here."

Mom snorted. "Peter, you can't even take care of your socks," she said. I could tell she wasn't softening.

"But Matt has a dog. Matt doesn't take care of his socks," I said. Matt was my best friend.

"That dog is a prime example of why we are not getting a dog," Mom said.

I thought she was being unfair. True, Pluto was a bit of a pest. He ate the Simpsons' furniture. And he bit people. But he was still a good dog, basically. Matt boasted about him all the time, and brought him everywhere. Sometimes I got a little jealous.

On my birthday, my dad came home carrying a box poked with holes. It was way too small for a puppy — or was it? Maybe he'd got me a puppy that was born just two days ago? "Dad!" I shouted.

Then I heard a soft small noise coming from inside. It was no kind of a bark. It sounded more like — a meow?

Dad reached into the box and lifted out a tiny orange furball. "She's all yours," he said with a grin. "Happy birthday!"

The furball quivered in my hands. I tried to hide my disappointment. A cat? When did I ever say anything about a cat?

I had picked out a dog name years ago. Toby — as in October, my birthday month. The furball had to be called something.

Mom and Dad liked Toby because she didn't need to be walked, and she didn't eat furniture the way Pluto did. But they liked her for other reasons too, reasons that weren't practical. I could tell. So did I, despite myself.

Toby was no dog, that's for sure. But for a cat she was pretty cool. She made us crack up about a hundred times a day. There was the way she stalked around the house like a tiger, for one thing. Or how she'd fall off the table, then act as if she'd done it on purpose. Or how she'd try to catch a fly in midair, miss, and then pretend she was just stretching.

It wasn't just the clowny stuff, though. Toby was a pal, even though she wouldn't walk me to school, the way Matt's dog did. She wouldn't fetch a stick either, or bound over and knock me down so she could lick my face.

"What *does* she do?" Matt asked. "Cats are good for nothing, if you ask me." I never asked him.

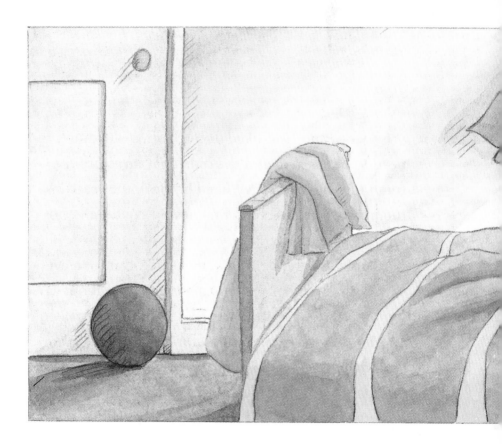

Toby slept on the end of my bed every night. When winter came, she slept on my feet to keep them warm. I don't know how she knew to do that. But she did. When I didn't get picked for the baseball team, I went into my room and shut the door and fell on my bed and cried. Then Toby started rubbing against my face, and her tail tickled me. I couldn't help laughing.

She always did stuff like that. I couldn't explain that stuff to Matt. I don't know why.

Over the next year, we watched Toby grow from a kitten into a cat. After a while, it was impossible to imagine life without her. When my next birthday came around, I didn't even ask for a dog. Toby wouldn't like it. And it was her house now.

A little while after I turned ten, Matt got in a bad accident. He was riding his bike and got hit by a car. One of his legs and his hip got all messed up. He was in the hospital for a long time, and for a while I couldn't even see him. Then he got moved to another place, called a care center. They were supposed to help him learn to walk again.

Matt seemed so different when I went to see him. I couldn't figure out if he was sad, or mad, or both. He told me he hated being in bed all the time. I think he was scared about his leg, too, and whether he'd ever be able to play soccer, or even walk. But he wouldn't say so, even to me, his best friend.

I think he missed school, too, but he wouldn't say that either. He did keep saying how much he missed Pluto, though.

That's when I first got the idea. "Why don't we bring Pluto in to visit Matt?" I asked my dad when he came to pick me up.

Dad laughed and said, "Are you nuts? Those kids in there are hurting already. The last thing they need is to get their arms bitten off." I guess he had a point.

"What about Toby, then?" I asked. "She loves people. I bet Toby could cheer Matt up."

Dad was quiet for a minute. Then we both burst out laughing, just thinking about it. "Let's find out if animals are allowed," Dad said.

We asked Maria, the nurse who took care of Matt. She smiled when we said we'd like to bring Toby to visit. "I think Matt would love that," she said. "He's always going on about that dog of his. But Pluto sounds a little too — umm — excitable for this place."

"Animals are okay, though?" Dad asked.

"Sure!" she replied. "We love having animal visitors. We've had all sorts over the past couple of years. Dogs, cats, rabbits too. Once we had a goat. Some other places have had llamas, horses, even chickens!"

"How can chickens make people feel better?" I asked.

"You boil them up and make them into soup," Dad said.

Maria frowned at him. "Scientists have found that animals can make sick people get well faster," she said, looking at me. "Cats, dogs, even *chickens* — almost any animal that's comfortable around people. They all seem to help people who are healing, or dealing with a handicap, or going through a tough time. Just petting an animal can make people feel less worried and less lonely." I knew that was true.

"You can see it happening," Maria continued. "When patients pet the animals, their whole mood changes. And animals don't just make people *feel* better — they can really help them *get* better."

"Well, *I'm* not having any luck making Matt feel better *or* get better," I said, kicking at a speck of dirt.

"Don't blame yourself," Maria told me. "Sometimes patients feel helpless. Or they think you're bored with them. Or they're a little mad at you because you are well and they aren't. Or they're just scared.

"That's one of the reasons animals are so helpful. Animals don't care how we look or how we act. They love us no matter what. And that means they can make people feel better even when friends and families can't."

I thought about all the times Toby had done that for me.

Maria handed me a sheet of paper. "Here are some rules to read before you bring Toby in for a visit. For one thing, she'll have to take a bath before she comes in."

Dad and I looked at each other and rolled our eyes.

"It's a rule," she said with a shrug. "No bath, no visit. She'll have to get a checkup too. Plus, Toby needs to behave herself when she's here. Just like you do."

I was starting to worry. Toby was a great cat, but she wasn't so good with rules, except the kind she made and we followed.

A couple of days later, Dad and I took a very clean Toby to the care center to visit Matt. I hoped no chickens would be visiting that day.

When we got to Matt's doorway, I put Toby on the floor so she could get used to the place. But before I could say more than "Hi" to Matt, Toby had jumped onto his bed.

"What in the — " Matt started. "Your *cat*?"

"Yeah. Toby," I reminded him. "I thought it might be fun to have her around for a while."

"I don't even *like* cats," Matt said, as Toby nuzzled his neck.

I decided to give Matt some time to change his mind. So I went downstairs to get some magazines. When I came back, Matt was nowhere in sight. Neither was Toby.

"Hey, we're down here, man!" Matt shouted. He was speeding down the hall in his wheelchair, Toby on his shoulder. Several other kids were following behind. "This cat isn't so bad after all," he said. "She's cracking everyone up."

I followed Matt as he wheeled into the lounge. Other kids gathered around to pat her as she draped herself on Matt's arm. She lapped up all that attention like a bowl of cream. I could tell Matt liked the attention too.

When we finally left, Matt made us promise to bring Toby on every visit. "She's pretty cool — for a cat," he said, giving her one last belly rub.

On our way out, we saw Maria. She told us about a special program that trains people and animals to work with patients, one on one.

"Different people need different kinds of attention," she explained. "Some like animals who clown around and make them laugh."

"Toby can do that," I said.

"Others want an animal to pet and cuddle," she said, "so they feel less lonely."

"Toby can do that," I said.

And she did.

THINK ABOUT THE SELECTION

1. Do you think Peter's parents are right to give him a cat instead of the dog he wanted?

2. How does Toby make Peter and his parents laugh?

3. How does Peter help make Matt feel better?

NOTING DETAILS

Copy the web on a piece of paper and write details in the ovals that support the main idea in the box.

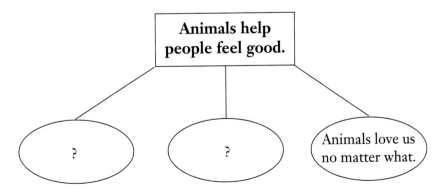

Animals help people feel good.

? ? Animals love us no matter what.

47

Trevor from Trinidad

by Delores Lowe Friedman
illustrated by Ann Boyajian

Strategy Focus

Trevor is starting school in a new country. As
you read, ask **questions** about how Trevor
is getting used to the change.

Until he was ten years old, Trevor lived in Trinidad, an island in the West Indies. Trevor's mother died when he was four. That same year, his father left Trinidad to find work in America, and Trevor went to live with his grandmother. His father called long distance, and Trevor sent him lots of letters. At first, his grandmother wrote the words, and Trevor drew pictures and signed his name. In every letter, Trevor said he couldn't wait until he could go live in the United States with his father.

Finally, Trevor got the call he was waiting for. It was time to move to the United States! His father had a good job, he had married again, and Trevor had a new stepsister named Samantha.

On his first day of school in his new country, Trevor wore blue jeans. Samantha had insisted on them. She said she would not walk with him to school unless he dressed "normally." In Trinidad, everyone looked the same in their school uniforms. There, he didn't have to worry about standing out.

"Samantha, are you sure these clothes are all right?" Trevor asked. He spoke with the accent of his homeland.

"I told you to call me Sam!" she replied. "Next time you call me Samantha, I won't answer."

"But . . ." Trevor started.

"You look fine!" she said. "It's too bad you don't *sound* normal."

"What's not normal?" Trevor asked.

"Oh, never mind," Sam said, sucking her teeth. "That's your class over there. Oh, poor you! Veronica Bowen and Tameka Wilson are in your class."

Trevor stood behind the last boy in line. He pushed his glasses up on the bridge of his nose. He tried as hard as he could to blend into the background. The teacher had gray hair and a round, warm face. She looked at him  kindly, and then she looked down at a piece of paper in her hand. "And your name is . . . ?" She looked up at him again.

"My name is Trevor Rainford, mum," he answered.

"Did he say MUM?" whispered a girl to his right.

"You must be the young man from Trinidad," said the teacher. "Nice to meet you, Trevor. I am Ms. Ruskin."

Trevor felt all eyes on him. The children whispered and pointed. His hopes of blending in were dashed.

Ms. Ruskin wrote her name on the board, and then she showed Trevor his seat. She asked all the children to introduce themselves to him. One by one, they called out their names. Trevor couldn't remember any of them. Then Ms. Ruskin asked, "Why don't you come up and tell everyone a little about yourself, Trevor?"

Trevor walked slowly to the front of the class. He remembered his teacher in Trinidad scolding him about speaking too softly and not standing straight. So he stood up as straight as he could, and in a strong voice he said, "My name is Trevor Rainford. I come from Trinidad. That's an island in the West Indies. It is close to the equator, so it is very hot. I like to read, draw, and paint . . . ."

Tameka giggled. "He talks funny," she whispered loudly to Veronica.

"He's got an accent," said Veronica.

Trevor heard them. "Where *I* come from," he said, "*you* are the ones who have an accent."

"Trevor has a good point," Ms. Ruskin said. "Now I'd like all of you to make Trevor feel welcome. Russell and Juan, I'd like you to show him around today."

The two boys looked over to Trevor and waved. At noon, they ate lunch together, and then Juan asked Trevor if he wanted to play ball. Trevor nodded his head happily. "I play football," he told them.

"In the spring we play baseball, not football," Juan said.

"Oh come on, let's play football with him today," Russell said cheerfully. The three ran outside. The equipment teacher helped Russell dig out a football. Russell threw it to Trevor. Trevor just stared at the oddly shaped ball as it hit him in the chest.

"That's not a football," he said as the ball hit the ground. He watched it bounce this way and that.

When they got back to the classroom, the boys told Ms. Ruskin what had happened. She smiled and said, "Of course. In Trinidad the game we call *soccer* is known as *football*."

Ms. Ruskin looked thoughtful for a moment. Then she told the class, "I have an idea. I'd like every one of you to do some research. Find out about where your family lived before they came to the United States. Ask your parents and grandparents, or anybody who can help. Try to learn about foods, games, songs, and dances — anything that made that place special. Next week, you can tell the class what you have learned."

A few days later, Sam and Trevor were doing their homework when Sam blurted out, "Veronica Bowen says you are stuck up."

Trevor began to doodle on the blank sheet of paper next to his math homework. Ms. Ruskin had said he was a good math student. He just needed to learn how they did long division in America.

"I don't think much of Veronica," he replied. "And I don't care what she says. She spends more time talking and giggling than she does studying. In Trinidad, Ms. Crown would . . . ."

"Trinidad, Trinidad! That's all you think about," Sam said.

"I like thinking about Trinidad," Trevor answered quietly. "I miss the beach, and I miss my friends."

"If you were in Trinidad right now, what would you be doing?" asked Sam, her voice suddenly kinder.

"Right about now, Granny would be making costumes for Carnival," he remembered out loud. While his grandmother sewed, he used to sit on the porch, doing sketches. The walls of his house were covered with his drawings and paintings. Many of the carnival dancers and musicians came in and out of the house, trying on their costumes and telling him how good his sketches were.

"Well, there's no Carnival here," Sam snapped.

Trevor didn't notice her impatience. He was caught up in happy memories of Carnival season. Carnival was part of him, and he was proud of it. He loved the music, the dancing, and the celebration. Best of all, he loved being in the middle of it all.

60

The next day in class, some children gave reports on the countries their families came from. Miko shared stories about Japan. Then it was Veronica's turn. Like Trevor, she had roots in the West Indies. Her grandfather was from Jamaica. She brought in tropical fruits for the class to taste. "These are mangoes, and this is a coconut," she said. "And this is . . ." She looked blank.

"A papaya!" Trevor offered. Veronica smiled at him and continued her report. He drew a mango tree and a papaya tree in his notebook.

After the reports for that day, Ms. Ruskin had an idea. "What if we turn everything we're learning into a play?" she asked the class. "We'd have to write a script, and make costumes and scenery."

"Yes!" the class shouted. Trevor's eyes sparkled with excitement.

"We'll wait until all the reports are done. Then we can begin to work on the show," said Ms. Ruskin. "Those of you who have not given your report should bring it in on Monday."

That night, Sam started setting the dinner table while Trevor doodled. Sam looked at his drawing. "Whatever that is, would you please move it so I can set the table?" she asked.

"It's a costume for Carnival," Trevor explained.

"It's very nice. Now move it," Sam said.

Trevor's stepmother, Joyce, laid a platter of curried chicken on the dinner table. It looked delicious. But Trevor had no appetite.

"Trevor, why aren't you eating?" asked his father. "Joyce made this meal especially for you. She called Granny to get the recipes."

"I'm sorry," Trevor said, and then he blurted everything on his mind. "I was just thinking about Trinidad. I have to do a report on it for school, and I don't know what to say. I mean, there's so *much* to say! How can I focus on one thing? Veronica did hers on Jamaica, and she brought in tropical fruits. But I don't want to talk about food, or games, or stuff like that. I want to think of something that will really show what the people of Trinidad are like. Then maybe everyone will understand *me* better, too."

"Why don't you do a report on Carnival?" offered Sam. "You can use your drawings and paintings to show what the costumes look like."

"And we have some great Carnival music," Trevor's dad added.

Trevor hadn't expected Sam to come up with such a good idea. She usually spent her time making fun of him. But Carnival was the perfect topic! When he described it to his class, they would see how wonderful Trinidad is and all the reasons he missed living there.

Over the weekend, Trevor wrote his report. He made colorful paintings of costumes. He sketched the steel drums the musicians played. Then he chose one of his father's records to play. He called his report "Carnival in Trinidad."

Everyone listened closely to Trevor's report. Their eyes lit up as he showed them his drawings. When he finished, the children applauded.

Veronica raised her hand and told Ms. Ruskin, "Trevor should do the scenery for our play." Juan and Tameka nodded in agreement. Ms. Ruskin smiled. "Trevor, would you like to be our scenic designer?" she asked.

"Yes!" Trevor answered excitedly."

On the way home from school, Sam asked, "How'd it go today?"

"Great! They asked me to design the scenery in the class play," said Trevor.

"I figured they would, Trevi," Sam said.

When they got to the front door, Trevor said, "Samantha, did you call me Trevi?"

"I just heard Veronica call you that," said Sam with a smile. "I think she likes you."

Trevor said nothing. He might as well just accept his clever "pain" of a little sister. There had been nobody quite like her in Trinidad.

Responding

Think About the Selection

1 Why does Trevor have trouble when he moves to the United States?

2 Why does Trevor's teacher have the class do research on their backgrounds?

3 Compare Trevor's school in Trinidad and his new one.

Compare and Contrast

Copy the chart. Read the description. Put a check where the description fits.

Description	Trevor	Friends at School
calls the teacher "mum"		
wears jeans to school		
calls soccer "football"		
likes to be in the school play		
shares things about other cultures		

Upstate Autumn

by Jed Mannheimer
illustrated by Mark Elliott

Strategy Focus

Melissa and her dad use e-mail to keep in touch. As you read, stop to **evaluate** what happens.

September

To: Dad@worldwork.edu

Hey, how have you been? I just set up my new computer. It isn't as cool as yours, but at least it works.

Mom is reading right now. She doesn't seem homesick for the city at all. She seems happy with her new job at the college library. I'm not happy with anything — except how pretty it is up here. You know, we're right on a lake!

But I miss you and my friends. I'm worried about starting school tomorrow. I won't know anyone! E-mail me soon. Love, Melissa

To: Melissa@eduplace2.com

Hi Sweetie! Loved your e-mail. Don't worry, I'm sure school will be better than you expect. If I know my girl, you'll have a flock of friends in no time. What's your teacher like?

I just got e-mail at home. I needed a separate address for my personal e-mail. Now it will be easier to stay in touch with you.

To: Dad123@eduplace2.com

My teacher is Ms. Lovejoy. She's okay, but she always goes on and on about outside reading. She wants us to spend all our free time in the library. Maybe if they had computers in the library, I wouldn't mind going.

Actually, maybe you could talk to the librarian, Mr. Smitz, about that. He seems pretty nice. Hey, maybe your company could sell computers to the school at a discount, and then I'd have something to do when I go to the library! Love, Melissa

To: Melissa@eduplace2.com

Sweetie, I'll talk to your Mr. Smitz about computers anytime you'd like. I'm not sure about the discount, but do give him my work phone number. And by the way, there's nothing wrong with outside reading, my darling daughter. Or inside reading, for that matter.

To: Dad123@eduplace2.com

Your jokes are so lame! Love you anyway, Melissa

October

To: Dad123@eduplace2.com

News of the day: Mom and I actually did something fun. When Mom picked me up at the bus stop, she had a brand new pair of ice skates for me. She said the lake will freeze soon. It's not even Halloween yet, but we *are* pretty far north.

Then we went down to the lake. Nobody was there except for the duck family. Did I tell you about them? They are so beautiful — the male has a brown chest, green head, and red eyes! Mom told me they are wood ducks. I ended up watching them all afternoon. Mom took some pictures. I think I'll surf the Net tonight and find out more about them. And just to be fair to books, tomorrow I'll look in the library for what they have. It'll give me something to do when the kids in my class are ignoring me. Love, Melissa

To: Melissa@eduplace2.com

Mel, give those kids another week or so. They're just getting used to having such a gorgeous, smart, and sassy girl in their class. I know what you're thinking — he's just saying that because he's my dad. Honey, I can assure you that I am one hundred percent objective!

To: Dad123@eduplace2.com

Columbus Day was fun. In the morning, Mom took me to the library where she works, and then in the afternoon we went skating at the rink with my new friend Katy and her mom. When the lake freezes good and hard, the four of us will be out there slipping and sliding! Sad to say, the ducks won't be around to watch us. They migrate for the winter. Mom says they'll be back next spring.

Love, Melissa

To: Melissa@eduplace2.com

Mel, I can't wait to see you in your new skates! We'll skate at Rockefeller Center when you come in for winter break.

Mr. Smitz called me at the office today. He asked me for advice about buying computers for your school. He says they will have the money for a dozen terminals right after winter break! So when I drive you home after vacation, I'll meet with him, the principal, and a couple of teachers. Does that make you happy?

To: Dad123@eduplace2.com

You know that makes me happy. Thanks, Dad.

Now, you're not going to believe this. Mom is just as bad as Ms. Lovejoy. She thinks I should stay at the library after school to do homework. She says that I'm staying up too late getting all my homework done. You know how Mom talks — "You're losing vital sleep and energy."

So from now on, she's going to pick me up at the school library instead of the bus stop. And to make matters worse, we're going to have fish for dinner tonight.

To: Melissa@eduplace2.com

Not much time to write. Sorry about the fish, Shrimp. Do what your mom asks. She actually has your best interests at heart, even though it may not seem so to you at times.

To: Dad123@eduplace2.com

Please don't call me Shrimp. I've grown at least two inches since I saw you.

To: Dad123@eduplace2.com

At first I thought Mr. Smitz was kind of slow because he didn't know where the computer books were. It turns out that he's not — he's just totally focused on science fiction. But he likes to talk about *some* other stuff, like nature. He told me that swans stay "married" for life — did you know that?

So it's not so bad in the library after school if he's around. Besides, it's a good place for me, Katy, and our friend Tricia to hang out until our moms pick us up.

To: Dad123@eduplace2.com

Mr. Smitz is having us do volunteer work now. It's fun — all we do is put the returned books on the shelves and listen to Mr. Smitz talk. He tells us about all these weird books that he wants us to read. I told him I don't like science fiction, especially books about computers and robots taking over the world. I think computers and robots will help save the world, don't you? Why haven't you been answering my e-mails lately?
Love, Melissa

November

To: Melissa@eduplace2.com

I'm sorry that I've been out of touch, Mel. I've been swamped with work and have stayed late at the office almost every night this week! You sound like you're doing great. Mr. Smitz seems like an interesting guy. I'm looking forward to meeting him. I saw your old buddy Kendra the other day. She told me to say "Hi" and that she'd see you during winter break. Your ever-loving Dad

To: Dad123@eduplace2.com

Mr. Smitz says "Hi." He showed me how to find stuff in the card catalog. I promised I would teach him how to locate books on-line when we finally get computers. He likes deals like that.

I told Mom how nice Mr. Smitz is. I think she's going to invite him over for dinner. I just hope she doesn't make the poor guy eat fish! Love, Mel

To: Dad123@eduplace2.com

Dinner with Mr. Smitz was okay. We didn't have fish. We had pizza, my favorite. He and Mom didn't talk about librarian stuff, but that would have been boring anyway.

Then I had a nightmare that Mr. Smitz was my stepfather. I would never want him to replace you. I don't think Mom would want him to either. When I told Mom about it, she laughed, but then she said it would be a bad idea to tell Mr. Smitz about it.

To: Melissa@eduplace2.com

Your dream sounds disturbing. I can understand how something like that can be scary. But you know that no matter what happens, I'll be here, and you will always have a place in the city. Take it easy, and watch out for the fish bones. Much love, Dad

To: Dad123@eduplace2.com

Ms. Lovejoy says we have to write a three-page book report. It's due after Thanksgiving vacation. It's totally not fair! I know for a fact that they only have to write one-page reports at my old school. I guess I could write about ducks, but Ms. Lovejoy said she wants it to be about a book we haven't yet read, and I've read every duck book in upstate New York. Do you have any ideas?

To: Melissa@eduplace2.com

I'm chock-full of ideas, my dear, but I don't know much about books for fifth graders. Ask your Mr. Smitz and see what he suggests. (Just be sure to say, in your most polite voice, "No science fiction, please.")
Love, Dad

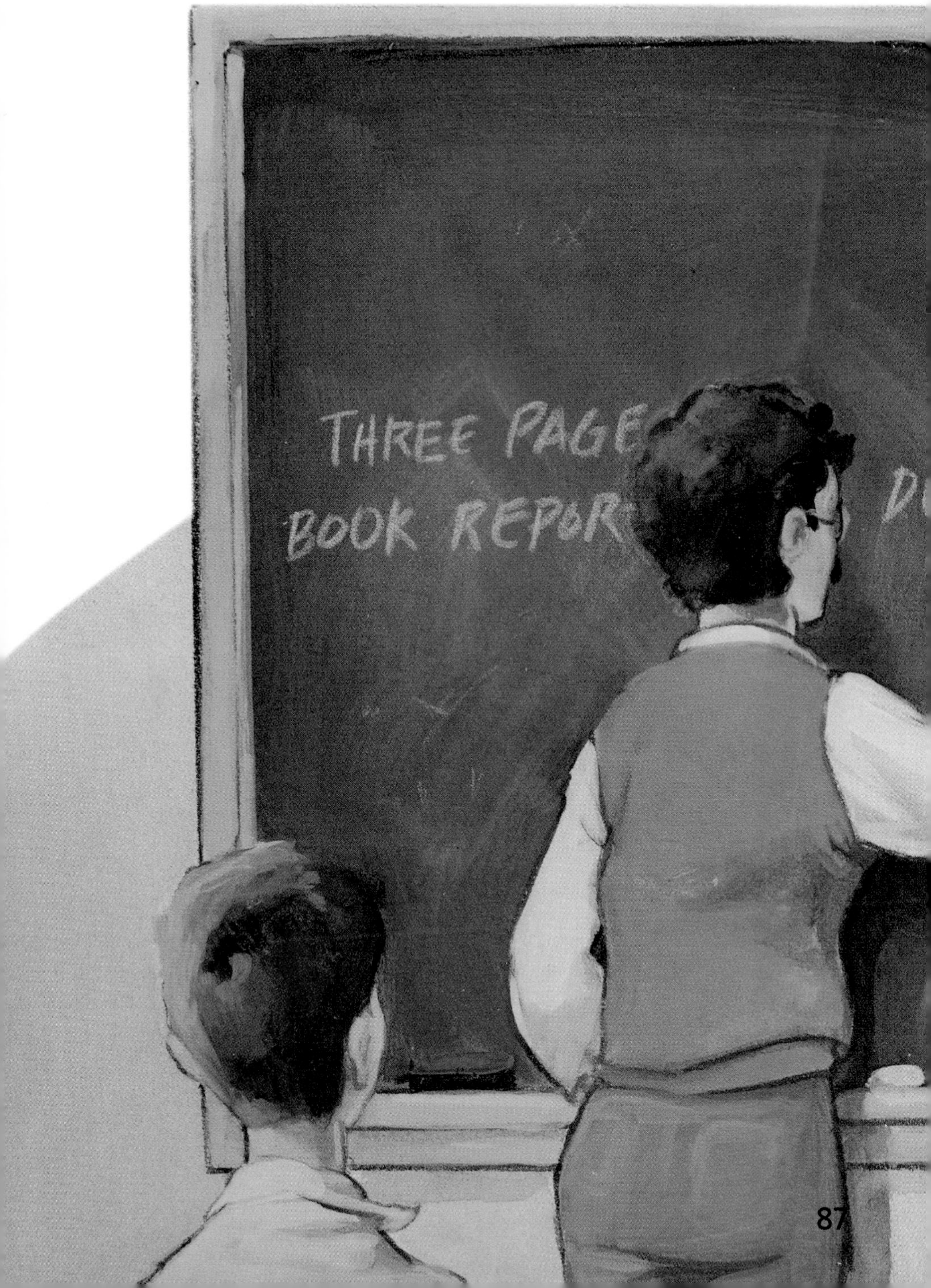
THREE PAGE
BOOK REPOR

To: Dad123@eduplace2.com

I told Mr. Smitz about how we e-mail all the time and it reminded him of a book he thought I'd like. And I do. It's about some boy who writes letters to his favorite author. So I finally have something for my book report.

To: Dad123@eduplace2.com

The book report turned out to be fun, believe it or not. The book Mr. Smitz recommended was awesome! And the report was a snap to write. Work sure is easier when you like what you're doing!

I miss you even more than when I first moved here. I want to know what we're going to do when I visit. There are so many things I want to do! Can we see a musical? I'd like to take a walk around the city and look at the holiday windows. And then see all my friends. And Grandma. But mostly, I want to hang around with you.
Love, Melissa

December

To: Melissa@eduplace2.com

I can guarantee that you and I will be a twinkling twosome. We can see a musical, maybe with Grandma. I'll be happy to escort you and Kendra around town as we look at the holiday windows. And how about the Bronx Zoo, so you can show me those wood ducks you've been talking about?

To: Dad123@eduplace2.com
I can't wait to see you! Love, Melissa

To: Melissa@eduplace2.com
Ditto, kiddo.

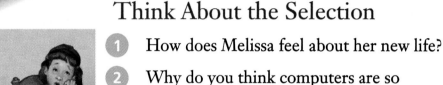

Responding

Think About the Selection

1. How does Melissa feel about her new life?

2. Why do you think computers are so important to Melissa?

3. What clues in the story help you understand why Melissa's dad thinks she's doing great?

Making Inferences

Copy this chart on a piece of paper. Read the clues from the story. Then write what you can infer from each clue.

Clue	What Can Be Inferred
Melissa says that she and her mom actually did something fun.	?
Melissa says being in the library after school is not so bad if Mr. Smitz, Katy, and Tricia are there.	Melissa likes company after school.
Mr. Smitz almost always suggests science fiction books.	?